GLIMPSES

Available by Brendan Kennelly

POETRY BOOKS

Cromwell (Beaver Row, 1983; Bloodaxe Books, 1987)
Moloney Up and At It (Mercier Press, 1984)
A Time for Voices: Selected Poems 1960–1990 (Bloodaxe Books, 1990)
The Book of Judas (Bloodaxe Books, 1991)
Breathing Spaces: Early Poems (Bloodaxe Books, 1992)
Poetry My Arse (Bloodaxe Books, 1995)
The Man Made of Rain (Bloodaxe Books, 1998)
The Singing Tree (Abbey Press, 1998)
Begin (Bloodaxe Books, 1999)
Glimpses (Bloodaxe Books, 2001)
The Little Book of Judas (Bloodaxe Books, 2001)

POETRY ON CASSETTE

The Man Made of Rain (Bloodaxe Books, 1998)
The Poetry Quartets: 4, with Paul Durcan, Michael Longley &
     Medbh McGuckian (The British Council / Bloodaxe Books, 1999)

PLAYS

EURIPIDES' *Medea* (Bloodaxe Books, 1992)
EURIPIDES' *The Trojan Women* (Bloodaxe Books, 1993)
SOPHOCLES' *Antigone* (Bloodaxe Books, 1996)
LORCA'S *Blood Wedding* (Bloodaxe Books, 1996)

ANTHOLOGIES

The Penguin Book of Irish Verse (Penguin, 1970; 2nd edition 1981)
Love of Ireland: Poems from the Irish (Mercier Press, 1989)
Between Innocence and Peace: Favourite Poems of Ireland
     (Mercier Press, 1994)
Ireland's Women: Writings Past and Present, with Katie Donovan
     & A. Norman Jeffares (Kyle Cathie/Gill & Macmillan, 1994;
     and Norton, USA)
Dublines, with Katie Donovan (Bloodaxe Books, 1996)

LITERARY CRITICISM

Journey into Joy: Selected Prose, edited by Åke Persson
     (Bloodaxe Books, 1994)

BOOKS ON BRENDAN KENNELLY

Richard Pine (ed.): *Dark Fathers into Light: Brendan Kennelly*
     (Bloodaxe Books, 1994)

BRENDAN KENNELLY

Glimpses

BLOODAXE BOOKS

ISBN: 1 85224 575 1   hardback edition
       1 85224 562 X   paperback edition

First published 2001 by
Bloodaxe Books Ltd,
Highgreen,
Tarset,
Northumberland NE48 1RP.

Bloodaxe Books Ltd acknowledges
the financial assistance of Northern Arts.

Cover printing by J. Thomson Colour Printers Ltd, Glasgow.

Printed in Great Britain by
Cromwell Press Ltd, Trowbridge, Wiltshire.

To Hugo Macklin

Yet sometimes glimpses on my sight,
Through present wrong, the eternal right.

— WHITTIER, *Chapel Hermits* (1851)

Survivors

Mugwort, Tansy, Ragged Robin, Shepherd's Purse,
Old Man's Beard, Honeysuckle, Dogwood, Stork's Bill,
Mouse-Ear Chickweed, Wild Angelica, Greater Celandine
like love
are with us still.

Cleaners

At four in the morning the women gather
in a cold place between the moon and the sun.
Their voices are the first singing birds.
There's a world to be kept clean
so that bright men still asleep
will foul it once again.

Game

Four plastic bags to bury
dead rats on the floor
suggest that though we're middle-aged
we're game for more

Expert

He scratches, giggles, sneers, looks, looks away,
hates eyes, goes mad, comes sane, reads
minutes of meetings till his wits are astray
again and he smells the bed where his mother bleeds.

Another art

Cut me down from four to two, she said.
She was happiest when she bled.
So he cut her down, he did.

Devotion

The grim beard is devoted to hate.
Out of that dark growth he will educate
the most caloried minds his squint has known,
devoted to the mobile phone.

Change

If I don't change I'll die, she said.
What part do you play in my blood?
I want a lover, sign of the cross on my head,
genesis in bed.

Wrestler

Sky, cloud, seagull, sparrow, men in blue,
unused chimneys, April branches, wet slate:
in 1943 I saw six-year-old
Bob McCann wrestling with the word 'Immaculate'.
Immaculate won, hands down. Bob scaled a rusty gate.

Butchers

The butchers whipped the herring through the town
and threw him in the river. Coming home,
they tied a dead lamb to a pole
decorated with ribbons and flowers
and marched through their butcher kingdom.
King Billy never dreamed such fervour.
If he did, it happened later.

Like days

God in heaven, is there anything boring as a meeting
where decent men and women sit
for hours that feel like days,
grinding the minds and arses off each other,
yapping shit?

9

Many years

My mother is twelve, dressed in white,
her right hand caressing
a greyhound's neck,

Johnny Harte has his hands
on her shoulders,
her sister Josie

is ready to dance,
her father Jack is not yet gored
by a Hereford bull,

her mother Ann stands broad and strong
in Ballyline light,
her brother Jer

kneels to life.

My child-mother is neat and slight,
it will be many years

until my father, dead,
touches, for the first time,
her dark head.

Small

A small knock on the door.
I wonder.
Enter.
No aisling can compare.

And now

'I should never have done it,' she said.
'And now that my daughter has grown
into a tall, beautiful presence
I know I am part
of the wrong man.'

Colours

She always picks the wrong man.
One drinks, one beats her up, one steals and lies.
The years are starting to laugh at her,
savage, mocking colours ringing her eyes.
This one hisses she has a putrid name.
If she chooses again, is it more of the same?

Wrong words

Don't tell me you can't remember
the hammer in your hand.
Ten years old, you flung it
at his head,
missed.
After that, he watched what he said.
Wrong words
stir Cain in the blood.

Old Sam

Old Sam was on the ball, she said.
It's simply a matter of waiting.
Godot and Manot know
the time for bed.
And when you wake up, please
tickle my knees
for a bit of a giggle.
That helps with the struggle
as dear old Sam knew well,
lyrical as hell.

The Shannon way

He's going blind. Wrote a poem once
after loving in a field by the Shannon shore.
He's recreating a rippling woman,
wants to believe in his mind but his eyes
tell him not to believe in his body anymore.
Will he listen to his eyes? Believe what they say?
In his head, the Shannon flows the Shannon way.
The rippling woman smiles and says she cannot stay.
She turns to go, calm and determined
as the Shannon flow.

Heartening

Is it not a heartening thing to see
an old man, his body shaking,
and realise that most days of his life
he raised his right hand in blessing?

Fresh

Night after night for sixty years he drank
pint after pint of Guinness, staggered home,
slept, rose, ate, worked, returned to the bar,
fresh out of the West, he said, like young Lochinvar.

Maggie and Paul

'Better marry than burn,' Saint Paul said.
Maggie Shelley answered that
if you're in love with a heap o' dung
you won't see a rotten straw in it.
Size up the men.
Bad shoes are better than none.

Of mouth and eyes

After he let her go
(some say she scarpered, against his wishes)
his mouth was a bag of ashes
and his eyes were pissholes in the snow.

Before

The tourist photographs the Cathedral
before he sees it.
Do we marry
before we see each other?

Bright

Sunlight on the Cathedral
is bright as an angel's eyes.
Did Swift know madness
looking at this?

Buttons

The beautiful, tall woman buys jewels
as if they were buttons.
The man at her side
pays. She
is a calm, magnetic presence.
She hasn't yet named the day
she'll be a bride.
The man pays and waits, opulent
and tongue-tied.

Free

Lost poems drift
like plastic bags across the sky,
get caught in a tree.
The tree is generous and lets them fly away.
Flying verse is free.

Hero

A one-legged pigeon fighting a crust of bread
is the hero of his dream.
If a goat's lust is the bounty of God
a glimpse is a vision in time's womb.

Ask

Did it happen at all?
I believe it did.
Are there documents to prove it?
Ask the dead.

Making nothing happen

Auden smiled and slyly said
'Yeats had a cold heart
and a warm head.'

Again

The blackbird in the April grass
is silent as a stricken wren.
I'd love to be strolling this way
when it sings again.

Recognition

What am I to make of the pusher's
resolute, dull, murderous eyes?
Would I give him a break?
How different is he from words
intended to cripple and wreck?
I look in his eyes, he'll never be broke,
he sells poison like slices of bad luck.

Otherwise

Sunday afternoon, Ballybough Road.
Children throw stones and broken glass
at each other.
Outside Duffy's butcher shop
are two small pools of blood.
Otherwise, a peaceful Sabbath, thank God.

Seat

The politician sat on the most
expensive seat in town,
relaxed, shat, pulled the chain,
himself went down.
He'll be up in time for the next election.

Soft spot

'When they pat you on the back, darling,'
smiled the politician's wife,
'they're looking for the soft spot
to stick in the knife.'

Across

Across three silent fields of summer
comes a call, a human and inhuman call.
If there's an answer
it escapes us all.

More power

'More power to your elbow,' she said,
'and your willy as well.
May you never see jail
the poorhouse
or hell.'

Battered

He sits in his battered Ford in the dark
outside his home. For hours. Why
won't he go in?
His wife has just given birth,
the stones are sniggering.
'Who's the father of the lad?' they ask.

The battered Ford accommodates a man
at home only in the dark
and blinding hours of work.

One dark cottage

The stars over the small houses
might concentrate on one dark cottage
where a woman flat on her back
is fucked by hate and rage
and there's no one she can tell
of her regular, nightly hell.
In ten years time she'll write to a man
in another country,
telling her story.
He will not reply.
He won't even send a Mass card
when he hears she chose to die.
The stars over the small houses
will not say why.

Parnassus

She took Patrick Kavanagh's poems to bed.
'Great company, lover and friend,' she said.

Breeding

'You have two choices with a fast bitch:
one is to breed her
but race her as little as possible;
the other is to race the legs off her
but don't breed her at all.'

At home

Love soars and dips
like the first swallow
at home in exile
over Doran's meadow.

Tablets

Lying, they disagreed. She argued him
through plump and slim.
'My love would give a headache to an aspirin.'

A third wife's observation

Stephen Gilhooley's third wife says
he's one comical man:
at night, after many pints, he loves
to piss under the moon;
come morning, he sneezes up at the sun:
the way he pisses and sneezes
are the signs of a comical man.

Paradise Lost

She phoned from Idaho, he was in Glin.
Forty years ago, a mortal sin
they didn't commit made love an also-ran.
Oceans apart now, they see
hell is the home of lost opportunity.

Never

Hate clings to his lips like sticky tape
that'll never let a fly escape.

Near

Two swans drift, arrogant and light,
near where the Bouncer drowned last night.

On

Katherine Woodcock died; so did her son.
Milton never saw either. He lived on.

Reader

He reads the new book, sees what's true,
knows the old writer through and through
but less of himself than he ever knew.
Does he read the book? Does the book read him?
Why is the old writer happy to be dumb?

A first glimpse

When love glimpsed me for the first time
I believed in God
though I was made of mud.

So far

'Ah! me jewel an' darlin' Dublin, me capital star,
only three murders this weekend, so far.'

Killings

He spent his time killing time
until time killed him. What's his name?

Conference

Twenty papers have been read.
Discussion follows.
Dinner then – a welcome break.
Later, in bed, two scientists
rediscover Einstein
after another bottle of wine.
He bites her neck.
In morning light
what is the meaning of a midnight bite?
What astral resonances shock
the mathematics of her neck?

Angel

The stabbed woman cries in her hospital bed,
'I can't believe my angel is dead.'

Closed Eyes

The right to close one's eyes
and be the seagull's flight
should not be thrown away
or forfeited
but guarded, guarded
against the lucid onslaught
of people in the know.

Children of darkness cherish
the old right to be
the stranger stopping you in the street
the football playing with young Luke's feet
the thought of snow
crossroads where killers learned to dance
words cudgelling each other beyond sense
stunted lovers growing with the flow.

Closed eyes affirm the right to know
why morning loves black night
or why a glimpse in darkness may tell more
than panoramas in the light.

Theft

Shy morning light, a snail's track
on the kitchen floor
is silver stolen from the bank of night.

Gifts

What does the blue Atlantic bring
this warm morning?
A seagull's feather, dancing
and a black, tiny fly, stinging.

More gifts

Who stands in the middle of the sick crowd
offering gifts of contaminated blood?

Range

The crow's croak has the melodic range
of morning in the Stock Exchange.

Informing the demons

Forsake me now
without a word.
I will tell the demons why
I'm bored and battle-scarred.
What the demons will reply
will spittle cold and hard.

The same

At the same door, the same word:
goodbye. Goodbye.
On the face, the lively smile.
In the heart, the sleepless cry.

Temple

On the catwalk stickthin
Lulu sells her hips
dreaming of a Hill of Tara
plate of chips.

Presences

love is present
love is lost
a boy is drowned
off the Waterford coast

love is lost
love returns
a father visits
a place of bones

Cain

I met Cain
in Grafton Street
he was smelling
yellow flowers

he was handsome
tall and strong
he would be
forever young

he loved the flowers
that lit his face
like a saint's
in the state of grace

before light decides
to crush or maim
and the dark agrees
to do the same

Your way

If you want to find your way through Dublin
follow that blind man. Let the sky
be puritangrey or fascistblue
the manic street will part for you.

Triumph

If there were no death
how would the world
survive the babble?
The grave is a hole of sanity.

The other way

Who turns in the street
and looks the other way?
Why is her hair dyed red
and yellow?
Why does she stop and stare
at the sky?
'Of course I'm mad,' she mutters upwards,
'I never lie.'

A time

There comes a time when
a perfectly balanced woman
will lie on a wall
and let the attentive sun
take all. She lies there, dreaming
of the sun's perfect sense of timing.

Slave

He is so enslaved by money
the smell of her skin
is the currency within
    and the touch of her hair
    is the wallet
    in his pocket.
Her love is what he'll spend
    in every weather.

Pilgrims

She wears the decades like pearls round her neck.
She takes them off at night
    and she is free
        so free
the pearldecades kneel before her
    like pilgrims on Croagh Patrick
        scattering a prayer
    to the ageless mountain air.

Fish

She said her cunt smelled like fish.
The Salmon of Knowledge, she added,
or maybe a cod
on a hot summer's night.

Scratchword

The word is scratched on a small stone
in the shadow of a rock:
epic.

Advice

'All you have to do,' the editor said
'is forget how to sing
and learn how to be
an instant expert
on everything
under over behind
or in
the sun.'

Gratitude

Knees and back affirm it was a frosty night.
Eyes, fixing on the windowsill
in early light, are grateful
for the neat, fresh gift of pigeon shit.

Evolution

Whew! I got here.
I mightn't have
but I did.

Getting to know

The man who lives in a firm shell
gets to know the snail well.

No softie

'Snail in the light, worm in bed,
but you're no soft mollusc,' she said.

Nakedness

The end of the human adventure
is the soul's nakedness
before God.

What I greatly fear
is my soul's nakedness
before anyone.

Mabel Street Commandments

A concrete wall spiked with glass:
Thou shalt not pass.

Sunlight on a Daycare Centre:
Easter.

Magic

Her speech was magic, the most magical bit
what she left out.

Late

I name the dead I loved and love
one by one, this Christmas night.
How late is it? Late enough
for candles to shiver and go out.

Literacy

Your face is a story, she said.
Read it, he replied.
No, she said, when it comes to you
I'm illiterate.

Goddess

In the succulent world, she opens each morning,
closes each night. This goddess knows
when to be wide, when tight.
Smart girls learn from the divine light,
heaven strolls along the canal
late at night.

No equal

His voice is money.
It has no equal
adores itself
is superior
to father mother
sister brother
whoever passes for neighbour.
It will bequeath to the future
a sound like no other
a sound like a hammer
in the hand of a man
announcing to faces

all defeated but one

'Gone!'

She

works, rears children, is never paid.
When did she walk a street
with little to do
like you or me?

Best

When the body is so tired it can't record
what the mind has to offer
it's best to drown into a dream
let dark rich nothing take over,
thrashed victim, unspeakable lover,
dominant as ice or fever.

Up from

Up from the steets thrills her voice,
'Romeo! Romeo!'

Why won't he open the window?

Revelation

He had a peek at the arms dump,
saw the bodies of men, women,
children. The sun shone,
revealing forgetfulness.

As you will

She turns her face to the sun
like a flower
or a child craving mercy
from the one and only man.

Half-afraid

Sometimes, the moon is mockery
sometimes, love.
Dan Kearney likes to consider it
when he's smoking his pipe.
Dan thinks the moon is a cautious old biddy
half-afraid to smile.
That half-afraid thing makes the moon
interesting, Dan says.
That half-afraid thing is the moon's style.

Half-afraid like myself at times.
Half-afraid like lovers facing the thought
of being together for life.
Half-afraid, no more.

The other half of half-afraid
opens many a door.

Now

Open the window now
   let the trees come in
      let them walk around the room
         look at books and pictures
         then drift away
leaving behind
         a dancing heart
a wideawake mind.

To ladies

Sign in a pub in Mullingar:
'Ladies must not have children in the Bar.'

Welcome

At the front gate of Trinity College
Sebastian Alfred Gillespie
is showing his ancient Celtic penis

to tourists
whose time is limited
and are eager to bypass

all such spontaneous sights and smells
for a quick peek
at the Book of Kells.

Expert

After cutting the heads off the eels
he piles them neatly into a stack.
How would these expert hands respond
if a harpoon ripped into his back?

Signs of signs

To have been bitten once by a dog is quite enough.
It happened that day in Isleworth
when I strolled into a café for a cup of tea.
Nobody there, except this dog that looked at me,
bit me to his satisfaction, and retired. I ran,
noticing on my way out
the sign 'CAFÉ CLOSED'.
Since then, prompted by a scar,
I look for signs of signs everywhere.

A pair o' them

Old bard, young bird:
In the end will be the word.

Long enough

How long did Homer stay in Purgatory?
Long enough to tell
James Joyce about the shackled odyssey
your man in the street must make through hell
till he stumbles on his wife in bed,
a calm storm of thoughts unfullstopping her head.

Searcher

He searched at home. Nothing doing.
In a street in Rome, scarcely knowing
where he was, he found it.
A hint of light sets the cock a-crowing.

Learning to serve

The Minister for Hellth is arguing his case
that devils must be taught to know their place
in the proper corner of each political mind
where they will learn to serve the deep needs of mankind.

Forgiveness

That Saturday, he forgave them all their sins.
                              Who could blame the man
if he slept with a bottle of Jameson?
Four dark walls whispered pardon.

Transformation

Her scream of love ripping his head
made a bloody battlefield
of a bumpy bed.

Friends

The first time I saw Beauty and the Beast
Beauty was a sly hostess, Beast an innocent guest.
Years later, Christmas, memorable feast,
Beauty hovered, served the hungry Beast.
Later still, we met in different places.
I knew my friends, though they'd swapped faces.

The best worker

If the letter was not from America
the troubled look faded from his eyes
and for the rest of the summer day
he was the best worker in the place.

At ease

When she died he married her sister,
got on well, happy family,
haunted though he was.
They said he was most at ease
sleeping between a living woman
and a ghost.

The Radford scale

On the Radford scale
anger
of male and female
is only one letter
short of
danger.

Home

'No place like home,' she said,
      eighty in her rocking chair
'where you can spit in the fire
      saucer your tea
           and call the cat a bastard.'

Grunt

He'd lived there all his life, was over
ninety when he died
yet nobody there
knew how he'd lost thumb and finger
on his right hand
although the Pig Finley grunted about a night
on Banna Strand.

Making a living

'When a man lives in a city addicted to lies,' he said,
'he should be commended
        for making a living
            out of the eternal verities.'

Bleeding

Shame happens quickly, lingers long.
Both hands are bleeding
after twenty years, it seems. Remembering,
he bunches either fist, his mouth
a grim twist.

Repeater

I repeat myself non-stop, he said, because
nobody listens in the first place.

May way

The moon on a bright May day
like Winnie Bird, will have her way.

New wings

When heaven opens its pincer jaws
to bite a passing woman
her rhythmbody sprouts new wings
and flies cleanthrough the human.

First day

In the land of no rule, breasts and belly
up and up in morning light. Every day
is the first day at school. Learning
is the art of beginning.

Picking his way

James Joyce walks down a laneway
off Thomas Street this Saturday morning.
Seven lads were sick here last night.
A long time now, Joyce is blind
and yet he skilfully picks his way
        among pools of vomit
                reeking in the sun,

        with a neat black walking stick
                picking his way

elegant, slim, exiled and confident
        sniffing now and then,
                blind stylish man.

41

Miracle

in the bluegreen sealight of Donegal
    the brown rounded mountainous
        cheeks of her arse
    are a soft miracle

Procession

Wild Clare music is sad of a sudden.
    Love dies
and a thousand ex-lovers
    are a bleak procession.

The song

The song poured from 1939,
war was born, young men died,
sugar was scarce,
there was a bad black streak
in nearly every loaf of bread.

Wrong and right

He took the wrong flight.
When he landed in the wrong city
he had one right night.

Adventurer

The old priest back from Africa,
reads his breviary by the fire.
To be welcomed, respected, put away,
who will talk about the matter?
He knows Latin and, from a young man,
the wild adventure of being alone.

Surrender

All night long
he sang the riveting, rivering words
over and over
though he couldn't name the song.

He didn't need to.
This was more than art.
This was the willing surrender of everything
he believed he knew about his heart.

The ones

Have the dead a sense of humour?
What do they think
gazing on our human farce,
efforts to trap it in verse?
Are they the ones who know the ones
who deserve a kick in the arse?

Missed

He fumed from the kitchen.
She threw a knife at him,
missed.
His eyes are rainbow pain.
Hers are black frost.

No time

From room to room he roared and strode.
The children cowered in the bully light.
'Let him rant and rage,' their mother said,
'a barkin' dog has no time to bite.'

Every trace

You'd swear the bath was a pagan well,
     her god a loving boy.
         She slid down the side
till the water covered her head.
         She upped then with fierce joy
smiling at the boy. 'I want to wash
every trace of that bastard out of my skin,' she said.

Birth

where the Shannon meets the sea
in an island bleak and worn
piety sheds an e
pity is born

Hands

Close to boiling water spilled
over his hands. He looked at them.
They'd loved her, built a house, pushed a plough,
dragged seaweed from the rocks, floored
the bully Kinahan, made music now and then.

Burning now.

Styles

If God is a shout in the street
the Devil knows when to whisper.

Invitation

'Come hither ya Slither,' she said. 'Get yer lazy
back an' arse away from that wall.
Grab yer granny for a tango
while yer grandad has a ball.'

Day's end

For fifty years she has seen men drink
themselves thicko. It always comes to this:
men staggering home, herself at the pub door,
'I have yeer money, boyos, and ye have yeer piss.'

The moment

She knows the moment when every light
must be put out. Black freedom now.
Love and nightmare stride about.
Black freedom stages fright and rut
in mind and heart and gut.

Never stops

He never stops performing now.
Couldn't, if he wished.
He'll never ask, 'What have I lost?'
No need to.
He's cocky, won't be rushed,
the crowd is waiting, and the cheers,
and the betrayed, betraying years.

Mouth

To speak of an obvious thing
as though it were a stunning truth
is the privilege of one decent man
with an icelandic kitchen mouth.

A quiet mention

He bullied her for years.
One day, quietly, she mentioned a gun,
an uncle. Bully took the boat.
She ran the Women's Marathon.
She didn't win and yet she won.

Parting

'You bore me. I'm leaving you. Tonight.'
'Don't let the door hit your arse goin' out.'

From now on

The old woman asked him to wash her feet.
He did. She closed her eyes.
There was no one or nothing she couldn't forget.
From now on, there's no forbidden fruit.

Of geography

Northern ice in Southern sun
melts a little, holds its own.

Reading

when he's reading
he thumps the words
till they lie
bleeding

Gang

His shadow looks stronger than he does.
It stalks him with silent ferocity.
It summons other shadows to its side.
A gang of shadows stalks him now.
Dark, calm and bold
the shadow's silence speaks to him.
He listens to the speaking silence
as if he were learning catechism,
does what he's told,
his way of growing old.

Breath

She took his breath away.
Forty years later, she gave it back.
Grateful, he accepted it.
Equipped, he set out.

Margin

In the city of caricature and mocking distortion
Jimmy Dick McGilligan
begs and smiles on the margin.
His home is nowhere. It always takes him in.
He answered a bishop's questions once
on Limbo, Purgatory, excommunication,
mortal and venial sin.

Planners

Plough, star, sickle, hammer,
a million people frozen in homage;
in a back room of Dooley's pub
five men plan damage.

Lady Senator

The men about her are barking and biting.
She goes down shouting.

Passing time

He climbs to a high room in the Big House
picks one of his polished guns
looks out the window at the peaceful river
shoots two swans.

Only one

A big book, a very big book
read by some, admired by many
but only one gifted scholarly crook
knows the whole story.

Pleasure

'If she gets half the pleasure outa spendin' it
that I got outa hoardin' it
she's welcome to every penny.'

Ave

'God love yez, professor,
yez look like yez could do
with a bit o' tax relief!'

Tickle

A prosperous light
on a poor face.
Dark evening clouds
are not out of place
in a trueblue sky.
Three politicians contradict each other.
A youngster killed by police
may sue through his mother.

Gentle May rain starts to fall.
It tickles me to know
I know
nothing at all.

Ninety-six

Swedenborg's angels dance, advance
towards the dayspring of their youth.
I know a woman of ninety-six
a gummy crackling beauty

who says 'A lighthearted woman lives long,
lets no bully enter her house,
sows in the Spring, reaps in the Autumn,
won't stop a plough to kill a mouse.

God's help is nearer than the door,' she says.
'Work is better than talk.
Make sure the bed is fit and ready
when you take your lover for a walk.'

Necessity

We'd best be ecumenical.
The Cross is too big for the hill.

Swift

Caged in a Cathedral he
lashed others to be free.

Twist and turn

He backs her up against the door.
'Be my virgin, be my whore.'
'I'll be your every twist and turn
so long as you show me a happy horn.'
Midnight streets sing love is born.

Touch

Touch me, she said, touch me
there, there, there.
I'm a jigsaw, chessboard,
ludo, snakes and ladders.
Play fair.

Living with limits

The giant water bug of the Southern United States
can copulate 100 times
in 36 hours.

Members of our Men Only Golf Clubs
have more limited powers.

Education

Bifurca, a species of fruit fly,
has a body length
of 1.5 millimetres
but produces sperm
58 millimetres long.

I recall a time
when such a marvel
would be immortalised in song.

That same fruit fly's sperm
contains a poison-like spider venom
damages the sperm of any other
male it may encounter.
This sperm is also toxic to the female:
the more often a female fly copulates
the shorter her life span.

A fly may educate a man.

Friends

I glimpse a black cloud
with a white cloud on its back
and think of one friend
scarred by love
and another
whose heart refuses to break.

Jobs

No more killings, he said.
I'll try teaching instead.

Gail Shannon's prayer

Lord, I don't need another mountain.
Just send me
a decent man.

Miss

      A narcissistic glance
in a shop window
      means she misses
      the stalking shadow.

The coldest place

When words knife through you
and you pretend to be
unbloody and unbowed

       why does it help

to sit in the coldest place you can find

       and say the stabbing words aloud?

This fun

Two rats play with each other
in deep weeds of the canal.
This fun
inspires a passing human.
It's a long time since he saw people
enjoying each delightful ripple

and longer still since gratitude
played in his blood.

Proximity

'He's the biggest fool in the place,' she said.
'That's why
he's nearest to God.'

Suppose

Suppose the entire venture
    is
        one
            long
                lie.

Sometimes it's a privilege
to sit and listen to a seagull's cry.

Fridge

Fridge humming at three in the morning
brings Annie Carney

                    swaying and singing.

Forget the pain.
It's time for apple juice
fresh from Eden.

Flow gently, sweet Afton

As Gandon walks the field, smoking sweet Afton,
repeating Lucy Finnegan's name
he finds that he is holding his breath
from time to time.

Giggle

If this coastal erosion continues
we'll all be wondering where
are Donegal Galway Kerry Clare
and the ghosts of tourists
will giggle to see

where dear old mocking Dublin
used to be.

Transformation

They sailed from Cobh with a skeletal crew.
It took a hundred and fifty years
before the coffinship became
another QE2.

Say

The doorman decides who's allowed in.
The editor writes 'We', like the Pope.
You can hang more people with words
than you can with a strong stretch of rope.
Walk through the empty house. Say despair. Say hope.

She says

She says the syringe is not her own
She says the knife is for her protection
She says she was reared in the shadow of Jim Larkin
Who respected the dignity of men women children
She says she is not afraid of prison

Father to son

'Crooked? He was so crooked, son,
everyone in Ireland knew
if he swallowed a six-inch nail
he'd shit a corkscrew.'

Strange feast

Went to war, returned, found peace,
love too, a while at least, lost
her, her laughter, songs, body warm and near.
Regrets nothing. Fought, loved, lost. Strange feast.
Likes to walk the streets now, and the desolate beach.

Page one

When the anger at grammar had subsided
and the notes on Swallow Street were done
he knew the future was a book and he tasted
the wondrous opening sentence on page one.

Easier

How peacefully he wipes the bloody knife
on his apron, scarred, so peacefully you'd swear
that chopping up a Wicklow lamb
is easier than chopping up a man.

Trees

I love it when trees lean forward or sideways
and talk to each other.
I think of my efforts to talk
to my dead brother,
his efforts to talk to me.
This morning the trees are leaning,
trembling and talking.
Love of trees is a long passion.
What do they think of men?
I talk to trees with my eyes.
I pray for my brother's peace.

Free

When he bends the knee is when
he cuts free.

Inches

On this grey day
love sleeps inches away.
Love at sleep is love at play.

Sand

Depending on how and where you lie
sand is a slippery bed.
On the Nuns' Strand, a spider climbs
her ankle skin knee thigh.
She does not protest.
Neither do I.

One thing only

The politicians shout bellow roar
about fraud corruption treachery.
On one thing only they all agree:
'Not me! Not me! Not me!'

Servants

'I dream, Ophelia, how I'd love
    to serve your body.'
'When you switch to golf, dear Ham,
    I'll be your caddy.'

Rivals

Green white purple blue
    of a pigeon's neck
rival the rainbow
    over Ballybrack.

Demons

There are those why say that pure wild laughter
can never be a part of art.
To work effectively, a demon
must live in a human heart.
When a serious demon lodges there
it's hell to kick him out into the open air
where there's always the threat of laughter.
Demons rarely look demonic,
sloppy, horny, rude or sick.
Mannerly types. Urbane. Know every trick.

The moment

speed of the mind
speed of the senses
love the moment
when lightning flashes
welcome the word
that sings and dances

Manbeast

A beast doesn't know he's a beast.
The more of a beast a man becomes
the less he knows of himself or his name.
Often, though, that same manbeast
is better able to play the game.

Ambition

'As a boy, he wished to be a comedian.
As a man, he chased votes all over town.
If he'd succeeded as a politician
Dublin would have lost a genuine clown.'

Your way

We grow ruder by the day.
It's necessary, to have your way.
Old legs get crunched. So what, they cause delay.
Dark and blond survive. To hell with grey.

Wall

The wall splitting the boys' and girls' schools
split young lives then, older lives thereafter
though in the smoky glimpses of a midnight pub
the wall, still standing, was a cause of laughter.

Where it's at

There's big money in elephantine art,
Asian elephants particularly
though Israeli elephants
are increasingly profitable.
It all started with a dog patting a bone
like Van Gogh fingering paint
with the delicacy of a saint
fingering holy beads.
This was followed by a cat
showing mouseblood on its nose,
a purring feline rose.
Today, however, elephants are where it's at.
Art is anarchy, darling. Hot shit!

Good luck

Birdshit on the window
is a sign of good luck.

Stammer if you must
but never get stuck.

Response

When I said I love you
to the tree
it shook itself
waved back at me.

One and only

Sincere words are not fine.
       Fine words are not sincere,
Try telling that to Lafferty
       when she hits the beer.

She knows Robert Emmet's Speech from the Dock
       wordperfect by heart
and delivers it with more sincerity
       than one associates with art

even when paint conjures bluebells
       or words a rose
or Robert Emmet's one and only poem
       that nobody knows,

not even Lafferty in the light
       of herself, a star
shining on that unwritten epitaph
       in Gallogly's Bar.

Lines

The lines at the corners of her mouth
       are delicate, ferociously strong.
How have they grown to be like that
       in one so young?

Old shagger

'If there were no killing,' the old shagger said,
'How would the living dead
begin to learn how to live again?
Violence animates the blood of half-hearted men.'
The old shagger quit the main road for a crooked lane.

1944

'Get out, Sheila,' he said, 'quit the place now,
keep your eyes down, dress like you're fat,
don't wash your teeth, spatter your skin,
you'll rip marriages asunder with hair like that.'

1945

When Joe Culhane eases the timber
into the saw's teeth
and the saw's teeth into the timber
blackbird and lark are drowned out
and the green bus, packed with youth,

emigrates.

Love later

If you can't make it tonight
    your love for me
    my love for you

will shannon through Summer and Autumn.

    Christmas will do.

Tap

The man beating the drum learned rhythm
from a tap dripdropping into a kitchen sink.
His beautiful African-Irish madness now
makes tribal dancing other than you might think.

Near a building

That sad summer, the loneliest thing
I saw was a swallow
with a broken wing

near a building (admired by Ruskin)
chosen to contain
the skeleton of a Limerick elk,
bone emphasising perfect bone.

Preference

'I don't mind a journey through Arctic wind
but I'd rather leave that man behind.'

Quick

'You'll have to be quick,' she said, 'eye on the ball.
Most eyes see almost nothing at all.'

Among stones

Sergeant Kelly leans across the counter
and tells Mrs Wynn of the poem
in the suicide note
left among stones on the shore
by Noreen Kilbride.
His voice goes low as he reads
'Tonight in the darkness my body
will lie in the tide.'

A six-year-old boy at the door
looks like he has nothing to hide.

Leaving Cert

'Thanks be to Christ it's over,' he said,
'I'm goin' to get locked outa me head.'

Relatively placid

The small red ball
balanced on a jet of water
has caused many a laugh
at the Summer School
where Professor Godfrey Pogue
after an argument
about the nature of vacillation
throws Professor Rex Hanrahan O'Toole
over the bridge
into the relatively placid
midnight waters
of the Garravogue.

O'Toole sinks rises sinks rises sinks
as though in doubt.
Several distinguished minds
from three Continents
fish him out.

Crash

He joyrides through all she has to say,
crashes into her goodwill.
They stretcher him away.
She picks herself up, after a stricken while
and slowly, as if saying goodbye
to a particular pain,
begins to smile.

Mocker

He makes good wine, relishes dregs,
prefers crutches to legs.

Again

That tree again.
All birdsong, this cool, beautiful, June night.
Near the roots, a patient, coiled, brown cat
waits for darkness to fall.
Prowl.

Vanity

Thank you for listening, for looking. I admire
much, and love some of what you do.
In my vanity, I believe I glimpse,
among shadows and changing lights,
something true.

Story

He told his story the best he could.
The story flowed through town and countryside,
into Big Houses, labourers' cottages.
It changed over the years but never died.
Nor will it die, no matter how sick or twisted.

Vow

'I will never deceive anyone again.
I did so once, to my eternal shame.
Je t'embrasse et je t'aime.'

Beans

If I weren't a stranger to myself, he said,
I think I might go mad.
If I went mad I think
I might be at home in myself
but I'm afraid to go mad.
Does that mean I'm afraid of home?
Better be a stranger to myself
and pretend I'm at home
like everyone else
saying hello when they glimpse me,
whatever that means,
Hell, O, let me not spill the beans.

All that time

After the killing, Tommy Antrim
went to bed for forty years.
During all that time he enjoyed excellent health
apart from occasional weird sounds
assassinating his ears.

Reflection

She reflected that when he'd be a corpse
and worms would be nibbling his arse
he might, stretched on the flat of his back,
consider the stars.

The truth

'What do you mean by the truth of bed?'
'No man can fake an orgasm,' she said.

Shaper

I love the strange men and women
arranged on the shelf
but there's no stranger like the stranger
shaping the self.

I see you

I see you, stranger, reaching out to touch
the leaf touching the window.
You want to let it in like a refugee
nobody wants to know
but it stays out there, trembling at the glass
where cold winds blow.

Here I go

I'll never get to know you, stranger,
though you live in me
move about in my blood
so calmly I wonder
what can I do
to persuade you to let me know you.
You resist all such advances
go your own way
silently telling me to do the same.
Here I go, stranger, come what may.

Scratch

Did Helen of Troy ever give herself
a Herculean scratch on her back
like Polly Doolin in Bewleys
scratching
with what must be delight
as she confronts
a mug of hot, black coffee
and a thick, buttered slice of barmbrack?

He is

The stranger has a black cross on his forehead.
He is downcast eyes.
He is a story he cannot understand
though he thinks he knows the difference
between fiction and lies.

Being there

The stranger set fire to me.
I quenched myself.
He smiled.
'I knocked twice on your door,' he said,
'There was no reply.'
'I'm sorry,' I said, 'I went for a walk.'
'That's no excuse,' he said.
'Anyway, I don't like excuses,
They make my skin crawl.
You're there or you're not there.
Be there when I call.'

Clothes

The stranger looks at his clothes on the floor,
doesn't fear the prospect
of being naked forever.
He once suggested to Patricia Cross
that his days and nights were a search for nakedness.
Patricia said that, given the Irish climate,
this was a laudable enterprise.
'Everyone here wears at least two masks,' she added,
'both in and out of bed.
Therefore, my friend, don't let your quest for nakedness
go to your head.'

Scales

Scrupulous all his days, Pat Nally
weighs sugar on the scales,
getting the ounces right.
The young mocker spits his words in glee.
Nally, eyes fixed on the scales, says
almost to himself, 'There are none so blind
as those who cannot see.'

Sleeping and working

Clever demons sleep in the mind,
sleep as if they'll never wake again
till with a fury hard to understand
they wake, strike, gut their man,
live as if they'll never sleep again.

Simple

A man will drink himself to death
and back to life again
forgetting what it means
to sleep, not sleep with a demon.
A man is longing.
A demon is waiting.
Hell is a simple decision.
The gates take only a moment to open.
Stroll in.

A rhythm

I know a man who is a cell within a cell.
He goes to jail in himself
serves his sentence
comes out
goes back in.
A rhythm can create a man.

When it hits

There is a craving
beyond words
which, when it hits
the heart and blood
and gut and brain,
can make a man
a slave to what
he loves and hates,
it mocks his will
bombs him
till he sees no
difference between
killing and being killed.
The sun has fallen.
The seas are still.
This is the calmest place on earth.

Miracles

Water for Guinness
spills from Saint James's well in Kildare.
One miracle begets another:
You're walking on air.

But –

He gets in touch only when he wants something,
talks a lot, pumps out the charm,
re-creates the delights of childhood
on a maggoty Connemara farm.

And then, 'By the way, there's something I'd love
you to do for me tomorrow night.
I know you're a busy man
but – '

Meaning

No money means no man.
Money means stylish poison
flooding radio papers television,
O but think of the good it can do.

Fuck the muck and take clean air
if you can find it anywhere.

Bearing withness

Weep with the star of gold
the word that cannot be translated
the leaf that never grows old.

Heartbeat

The heartbeat of a lethal Irish joy:
I mock I mock till I destroy.

Transformation

Sitting outside the small house near the orchard
she turns the years over in her mind
like the pages of the Dickens novels
she reads, re-reads.
She is transformed
by what she permits herself to find
and to discard.
Charles Dickens is a lifelong friend.
A few ripe apples are hitting the ground.
She cocks her head at the applesound.

Whispers

The stranger struts through my blood
whispering 'You're useless, useless!'
I whisper 'Change your tune.'
He says 'One day you'll know the meaning of praise.'
With that, he quits my blood for other places.
Why are his whispers so devastating?

No longer a name

She's no longer a name, she's a number.
She told me the number yesterday.
This morning, I can't remember.
The number's eyes are a laughing blue.

Almost nothing

'I see something in the mirror,' she said.
'It helps me to know what's going on in my head.
But you understand almost nothing
without a pen in your hand.'

If I lie

If I lie with the demon now
I'm happy to be enslaved.
Do I know anyone I would see
as truly free?
The demon sneers at my side, in my head.
I rise and follow the slave abroad.

If I were to utter

If I were to utter the curses he knows
I'd understand
the four holes in the child's heart,
the trampled rose.

Duel

I foresee a day when the stranger
and the demon will fight a duel
to the death of one or both.
This will happen in a calm place
with no one looking on but an old man
sitting on a cracked grey chair,
two summer flies playing in his hair.
This old man understands pain.
If someone is fatally wounded
he won't move or say a word.
He'll continue looking at the scene
as he feels the first touch of serene
April rain.

Squatter

The demon loves the scruff of the neck,
perches, clutches there,
bangs the head like a ball off a rock.

The pain he dispenses
havocs the six senses.

He likes to riddle the eyes
of everyone, everything.
See what I see, he says

squatting on the hill of sneers
filling the world with their echoes.

Up from the earth

Up from the earth the voices came,
　　　voices buried stripped years ago
singing weeds and grass, gravel and bones,
　　　lovers I cannot begin to know.

Voices of friends who died in childhood,
　　　Tommy Brassil of the gentle smile,
Nellie Connor who laughed and vanished
　　　into the earth in a fevered while.

Up from the earth the voices come,
　　　glimpses of spirits that live in me.
Why do they suddenly sound, then vanish
　　　into eternity?

Short story

Billy Bunter and Jane Austen
play ting-tong together and go wild.
The post-futurist philosopher
hates being a child.

By the fountain

There, by the fountain, where, a child, I cried
to see the fox stretched in its blood,
the stranger and the demon walk side by side.

Therefore

I'm alive, therefore I love Kitty Leitrim.
But more, I hope our friendship
survives our lives.

Heart

In the heart of Dublin, not even the long
manic shrieks of ambulance and Fire Brigade
can undo the blackbird's song.

Runny

'Death, thou shalt die' he quotes to himself
crossing the road into Kitchener's Pharmacy
to get a few packets of Immodium Plus
because his bowels are getting a bit runny.
And if there's one thing he hates
as he faces the crowd, chatting of love and fame,
'tis the gruesome thought of shitting in his Jockeys
at the same time.

As suggested

Do your best, she said.
He did.

Turn on

The blind boy is looking for his sight.
If he stumbles on it, he says he'll make
a strong, long-serving bulb of it
and turn on the light.

A tall wall

She sleeps easily, the village at rest in her thighs.
The boy slumps at the bottom of a tall wall
drinking tears and cries.

Three dreams

I dreamed that you were dreaming
of a morning bright and blue
when weeds nettles furzebushes daisies
dreamed of you.

Now

In Ireland now, why do so many
young men kill themselves?
If the Liffey became a river of money
would it flow towards a sea of poverty?
Why do mirrors laugh at girls
looking at mirrors?
Why is a rope a hope beyond no hope?
Why does the sea invite young hearts
with happy words like
'Good night, sweet prince, good night'?

Somewhat disturbed

He knows damn well he's not afraid
of the silence of the infinite spaces
but he's somewhat disturbed to find
the sight of her naked breasts
suggests what it might mean
to be out of his mind.

Cocky and weeshy

Cocky Robin hops out through the black bars
of Stephen's Green,
devours a weeshy fly,
hops back in again.

Crawler

The spider crawls into the Bible
comes to rest
deep in the Book of Genesis.

School

The stars are children going to school
in the comprehensive sky
trying to learn why.

Supervisor

The moon supervises, praises
lovers trying to find their way
through love's mazes.

A quick visit

Love dropped in for a quick visit
had a glass of wine and a slice of bread
then faced the road and the night ahead.

Coming out

Coming out of the cave
in time to escape the coming tide
she turns and says
'Frank, behave!'

Gumming

I asked Malachy Brandon, eighty-two,
what he'd learned from wading
through eight decades of Dublin muck.
'Love,' gummed Malachy. 'Love.
And don't give a fuck.'

Above and below

Water from the well
water from the tap
innocence flows underground
poison struts on top

Old Irish

The old Irish word for kiss
is drink.
When a man drinks a woman
he knows how stupid it is to think.

Just another day

Dear Dublin, you sleep tonight in a bed
of scandal, savage gossip, caricature, hate.
Is this the legacy of our dead?
Will the good word be always late?

Trouble

The moment the word was made flesh
dignity troubled human trash.

Never again

At what moment in that town
of degradation and pain
did he decide
never to speak a word again?

Is the night a slave?

Book, bag, glass, pen,
spider, fly.

Shriek of an ambulance
crazy to help.

Branches of chill silver
whispering
and a lone cat moaning
to kill.

Is the night a slave? Has it a choice?
Does the darkness know free will?
Is the river lonely? Has the prison a voice?

Book, bag, glass, pen,
spider, fly.

The colour

Look at the grass.
The sun explodes inside a leaf.
Four hundred refugees
drown in a sea of promise.
Take that promise, turn it to colour,
wear the colour about your eyes.
The silence is full of cries.
Look at the grass.

All day long

Dear God, it pisseth all day long
and so I thank You
from my heart
for Christy Moore

in sweet fierce rattle-the-rafters song.

Pebbles

The white feather clings to the bread
     in evening gloom
and the pebbles in my brain
are stepping-stones for the demon.

First times

The first time she saw the dolphin
she dived in love with it.
In the depths, however, she met the demon
for the first time.

Guards

Look at the yellow flowers guarding the blue gate.
No Parking, Day or Night.
Whose blood is that pooled in the street?

Midnight

Let the pigeons fold their wings.
Let me listen deeply to the river's dreamsongs
(no saving the poet from the high bridge hurtling).
Let not the darkness settle on quarrelsome wrongs.
Let there be a ceasefire of tongues
    and in the open dawn
        let me sing what I mean,
           mean what I sing.

Fellowship

At the bottom of Grafton Street
a scowl-eyed aboriginal
leans forward and hisses
in my face
'Arsehole!'

Yes, I can see your point
but if you don't mind
I'd rather not advertise the fact.

When he looked

Why, when he looked at her beautiful
forehead temples eyes nose mouth cheeks chin,

did he see a skull?

That evening

What the most beautiful woman God created
said to him
that evening among the rocks
may not be repeated.

Head down

He knows he can't play the flute.
The three angels over the Bank of Ireland
                              know it too.
But head down, he sounds it, sounds it
until passing pounds and pennies
drop into his hat
and warm the cold street.
When that gutsy non-player lifts his head
he'll have enough to pay for bite and bed.

Pollen

'...for God, Who gave us grace and harmony,
            made love out of a lonely sigh...'

                        Whose? Where?
And why this evening, with such
            pollen in the air?

Preference

Such words of wisdom he had, they just
poured out, he didn't seem to need to think
and when I asked him why
he wouldn't write his wisdom down
he said he preferred blood to ink.

Roof

Look! Two magpies are battling it out
on the roof of a famous library.
A third magpie, doubtless The Prize,
turns her tail to the squabblers
and waits, apparently without interest.

Beautifully indifferent
    she looks everywhere
        but at the warriors
            as she prepares
        to soar to heaven
            with the winner
and show her feathery arse
        to the loser,

poor battered beaked-to-shame loser
    lonesome on the roof
        of a famous library.

Progress

Yapping, he can't stop yapping,
sitting, walking on his own.
He is a mobile phone
here where men sit
and cannot hear each other groan.
Thank you, John.

Remember that evening when
you walked back from the Christmas pantomime
with Dilke and Brown
and had a disquisition with Dilke
about what goes to form
a man of achievement in literature?
What a glimpse that was,
and after a pantomime too!
Enough to strike silence into any prattling soul.
Off you went and wrote a letter to your brothers.

And later –
'After dinner we walked to Ambleside
down a beautiful shady Lane
along the Borders of the Lake
with ample opportunity for Glimpses
all the way.'

Yesterday, a man said to me
he dreads being on his own.
When he goes from room to room
in his own house, he carries
his mobile phone.

Progress is another name for now.
Yet when I try to imagine grace
I glimpse a young man, tiring,
who said he always made
an awkward bow.

Learning

Love sniffs and claws like a young rat
learning his trade
in the challenging weeds of the Royal Canal
and the instructive mud.

If you must

If you must choose, she said, between praise and blame
choose praise.
Praisewords keep soul and body young
in amazing ways.

Analysts

The Dublin night is a beard and a woman
sharing eight cups of coffee
analysing corruption.

Advancing

A bank yesterday
a hotel today
a prison tomorrow

About roundabout

Love your enemy.
Love, your enemy.
Enemy, your love.
Your enemylove.
Love your enemy.

Witness

Be with me, stranger. Enough to know
I cannot know you. Be with me,
live in my blood, mind, bones, eyes.
Give me what you've always given. Surprise.

Birth

Loving wild signs of orgiastic art
she sees Tom Jones, she hears Tom Jones,
her present, past and future shake,

her waters break
but not her heart.

Her daughter's name is Temple King.

Men are happy
trampling each other
to hear her sing.

94

Morning, night

Meet a red-haired woman in the morning,
go back home.
Meet a red-haired woman at night,
Spend all you've got.

Time is on its knees before her,
longing to adore her.
Help time up, give it a chance,
let it ask her out to dance.
Red-haired woman moving on the floor,
dancing time will never ask for more.

Different

Love is riven in Intensive Care
bleeding from back and breast
paying the price of choosing to dare
a byroad different from the rest.

Safeguard

He slipped the future in her mouth.
She sucked it clean,
safeguarding in her gut
what has yet to happen.

Bell

It is a hideous bell,
shrill, insistent, vile.
After a while
I don't hear it at all.

When it stops,
the chill, silent streets
are prisoners on release,
tempted by peace.

Banishment

The cliffs are battered like the people
Darkness knocks at the door and waits
No sleep for hours, long hours
My dreams have banished me

Special

There's a special poison to be found
only in Dublin.

It lives in words, in eyes,
is its own Paradise,

will never be lost
until all flesh
is dust.

Another choice

See that whitest cloud
in the bluest sky.
Uncelebrated days are days
we choose to die.

I only know I never pay
enough attention
to what is really
going on.

I could cry
when white and blue
go slipping by

unnoticed

by stupid me
making my way
through the gadabout city.

Blame

Don't blame the city, she said,
for the way you make it to be.
And who do you blame, good sir,
for the poisoned Irish Sea?

Builder

On the June strand, Emily Birdthistle
(with the help of a small, pink bucket)
takes several minutes
to build a castle.

She stands back and admires it then,
as do many passing women and men.

Watch

The child watching the woman watching the man
watching the demon squatting on the moon
is watched by the stranger, familiar
and unknown.

Inside out

Look at leaves turning inside out
in the busy wind.
It's like being sixteen, then sixty.
What was lost? Found?
Sixteen, sixty, sixty, sixteen,
green and white, white and green.
A mind turned inside out
is not what it might have been.
No use guessing. Pay the rent. Move on.
Or stay. Sit at the window. Look again.
Leaves turning. Stay. Move on. Stay. Move on.

Moving on

songs to sing
things to say

don't let the demon
get in the way

A way

down the steps and down the steps
of maybe yes and no she goes
to where the future in a sea
of screaming children flows

Blessing

Beyond the swimmers, the dolphin rises into light,
blesses our eyes a moment, then
plunges down where it belongs
amid seawords seasilences seascreams seasongs.

Seasong

I cut the balls off the tiger
and throw them in the sea.
As they sink they sing in depth

'Death is a matter of money.'

Sunday morning

Someone threw a red knickers on my roof last night.
People going to Mass this morning
stand and stare, feast their eyes a while.
Then they drift towards prayer.

No mercy

There's no mercy in the tide, she said,
be it calm or wild.
I saw Vincent Gunning over near the rocks.
Where is the blond child?

Silences

'I was there,' he said, 'the night the hitmen done in my friend.
I ran away. He lies in the silence of holy ground.
I sit in my silence, knowing it is not enough
to ask forgiveness of the wind.'

Best

The best plan
is the fun an accident has
with a cute hoor of a man.

The change

'The change from yesterday!
Wild Ireland!
Jesus, the sea is fillin' the kitchen!'

When I hear it

I know satanic music when I hear it.
So do the pink red blue ginger yellow-haired
warriors kicking each other in the gravelled yard
deliberately and very hard.

Playing around

lived
veil'd
devil

Gift of

While Nostrodamus fascinates with future doom
(is it Hitler or Hister in the rhyme
bridging the Danube and the Rhine?)
she licks the freckles on his arms
and lights a candle in the narrow room.

Aesthetic

If the creature stalking the poem
is a shit-eater
why shouldn't lilies sprout
from the arseholes of corpses?

Few origins are so normal and vile
as certain roots of the beautiful.

Chewing

I've never understood yet always loved
the words of the man who said
'Beauty will save the world,'
chewing a slice of Bewley's bread.

Pleasure

Listen to the rock breathing
its pleasure to the sea.
Though you are centuries away
you breathe in me.

Fun

A gang of boys and girls, loving fun,
kick a young man senseless, or to death,
in latenight fastfood Rialto.

One girl says, 'It's like a fuckin' video.'

Even more

Because Jim Hurtigan loves peace
they make a woman of him.
Standing at the yellow door
she loves peace even more.

Never again

Anger flashing in the fist, the stick,
lashes the boy's back.
Pity struggling to be born
is granted an abortion.
Take the bus, get on the ship
never get in touch again!
Go with the stranger, or go alone.

Cultivation

The crow's feather she tickled him with
made him a self-believing myth
which he cultivated night and day
to her amusement and his decay.

Resonance

When Protestants march down the Catholic road
Catholics say its beyond all reason
like the resonance drumming through West Belfast
when a housefly makes its last confession.

Warning

Dublin is gridlocked, Cork crippled,
Galway strangled. Please be careful
driving through Kinnegad:
there's a loose cow on the road.

In the know

Dead faces, voices come and go
The carpet is well swept
Crows and theologians know
Why Jesus wept

Concluding the revelation

'Would I be talkin' shite?'
'Ya might.'

Lizzy

'The Queen who taught us to read and write
our own language knew what words are at.
Let gallant fools die on hunger strike.
Thank God for the Brindled Cat.'

Neck

'He has a neck like a jockey's bollocks,' she said.
'And he goes to Cheltenham in bed.'

A different way

If she kept on walking now
she'd be with the dolphins soon
but she chooses cruel company
and a different way to drown.

Giftwrapped

black and gold
became red and blue
when the Atlantic evening
envelops you

Daisies

daisies at the door
day's eyes open wide
Eddie's friends escaped
Eddie died

Shift

If you suddenly shift
to where the cliffs end
you hear the sea singing
eternal beginning
in a way that may involve
your ending.

Three things

Three things puzzled Aristotle's wife:
wild tides obeying a calm moon,
the workings of bees,
the mind of her man.

Strides

Logic strides where the seagull's beak
ravages nutritive havoc.
Logic backs off from the sea,walks on
to herbal tea and irrefutable definition.
Havoc will do what havoc can
with what is left of flesh and bone,
shreds of crab or gull or man.

Bitchfight

No fellas here (they're watching, though,
delighted)
just girls
in a bitchfight, hell of a night,
cursing, dragging, kicking, trying

to claw each other's eyes out.

The nobody mind

Lost words, lost people
are buried somewhere in the mind
that belongs to nobody
who might as well be
all that we know
of grains of sand
helloing the sea, farewelling the land.

Learning

Tiny body, massive helmet, she comes each day
on the back of the bike, learning to swim
in the Atlantic. Powering home,
she clings to him,
limpet to the rock,
child to the broad, blackleathered back.

Promise

She seized the dream by the hair and dragged it
till it fell screaming on its knees
promising never again to invade her sleep
with the slithery turncoats of Euripides
or a midgety gang of tormenting fleas.

Harvester

The islandman says Aristotle had three sons.
They left home to seek their fortunes
while Aristotle stayed behind
harvesting the fields and seas of his mind.
With ruthless skill he scoured his head,
never heard of his sons again.
The islandman says none of them read
a single word of their harvesting dad.
Instead, they wandered their own ways,
other fields, other seas,
other out-of-the-way philosophies.

Earth and sea

Children screaming in the playful sea
watched by an old man on the clifftop:

old man in the earth, watch over me.

What he wanted

'He was the shyest of them all, shy, so shy.
He knew Homer like the road for home.
He went to heaven yesterday.
She's gone to represent the pair of us.
No fuss was what he wanted. No fuss.'

Lads

'Lads, apples for the horses.'
'Fierce worker, fancy dreamer.'
'If she could only remember what she rehearses.'
'Call me Homer.'

Drama

You give us everything, take everything back.
Thanks for the drama of give and take.

Composition

On certain icy nights I know
a song is wandering the sky
        composed
of a cool mind's lucid gifts
and a heart's most inarticulate cry.

This morning's mail

This emptiness has never known a sound.
I watch the needle entering my left hand.
Rachel Thornton sets her eyes on Iceland.
Every minute, across the world, a child goes blind.
Why leave these burning words unsigned?

Nearly

The most interesting aspect of complete fatigue
is bed
where deep, lost hours of mercy
effect the nearly resurrection
of the nearly dead.

A matter of technique

The most effective way, the starlet said,
to answer the questions
of a bully interviewer
infalliblised by a retchy Inquisitor's cough

is to look deep in the predator's eyes
and whisper sweetly, 'Fuck off!'

Question mark

He curls like a question mark on the grass,
his left ankle broken. This picture
is what you'll carry through winter
and never be able to explain
other than muttering to yourself
that there's nothing so unshareable as pain.

Outside the church

The blind woman at the churchdoor
lightens the pockets of fervent prayer,
counts coins dropping from God knows where.

His bed

When Government whiskey shags his head
and he can't manage a clear word
why does he stagger to make his bed
in the corner of a Hugenot graveyard?

September

Starlings gather in their thousands on the wires,
silent and dark, prior to flying.
On a cloth drying on a windowsill
a wasp is dying.

Not too much

Don't say too much, he said.
Mention the unanswered letters
lying on the floor, the two
or three books you really love,
the unutterable stupidity you feel
thinking of time, the way five
thrushes tilt their heads listening to grass
or what the grass conceals and offers,
how you cherish
standing with a friend
one autumn evening
talking of a night in Greece
when he remembered poems of war
and your voice offered to the stars
three songs of peace.

Changing style

'Our Irish style is changing,' she said,
'We've a new mode of attack.
It seems we prefer steel kicks in the head
to stabs in the back.'

Reply

If you ask me what will endure
(when all is lost) in this land of laugh and cry
I will reply
the black, shaggy art of caricature.

Headlines

Headlines shriek today, are dead tomorrow.
Their corpses fuck, breed shrieks of sorrow.

No answers

Who should be allowed to speak on air?
Why these hours of sick remorse?
Hate of earthrape some call progress?
Shove your pylons up your arse.

The fault

Love? Is it possible to kill?
Coffin, bury it in style?
I know a man who loves to kill a poem.
I love a man who said 'I have been working
with a vile old pen the whole week.'

Loved him as a boy. Love him still.

'The fault is in the Quill.'

Nightnight

Go to sleep. That's a strange sky.
Hard though you look, only one star
laughs at your scrutiny.
Hope the night passes without pain
or inexplicable, mocking nightmares.
Pretend you know who you are.

A different game

He broke his jaw, lost the sight of one eye
playing Gaelic. Who did it? He won't say.
He stands at the Corner of Talkers, not a word
out of him, eyes calm and hurt, face resolute and grey.
A different game then. Red and yellow cards today.

Style

The morning Larry Rainbow hanged himself
Mary Haley lost a clump of hair
Charlie Mackey hit the whiskey
Ted Lane got money from America
and Isaac Jones, walking greyhounds near tall trees,
found Larry Rainbow hanging there.
They all said goodbye to Larry
with a drink and a prayer.
This was the style he liked. This was what he asked for.

No meddling

Why can't we leave the Saints alone?
If Augustine was a randy lad when he was young
then let him be the randy lad he was when he was young.
What else drove Solomon to write his song?
A soul at ease has gone beyond all right and wrong.

A man

I am a man, he said, and therefore
do not consider
anything that happens to me
foreign to my nature.

Wisdom? Drivel?
Neither? Both?
Inescapable?

Wife and children

The man who called the stars his children
and the wind his wife

                    said he found
the first political duty a man should have
is the happiness of his friends.

Shortly before

One blue day, in the badbread years, a girl,
shortly before she befriended the sea,
looked over her shoulder
at my six years, eyes full of silence,
and smiled at me.

Path

The path risks going astray, leading astray.
Going this path needs practice. Practice needs craft.
Stick to the path, singer to the words of the song.
Learn the craft of thinking, unswerving, going wrong.
In spite of love and politics, a man
reaches the place that he can.

What's that you said?

Logos. Eat
through flesh, gnaw
at the marrow-bone.
There remains, and will remain, this darkness.
Wait for an angel
with a key to the abyss.
What will speak to us?
Listen to what is said.
The word is a house well founded.
The table is laid.

Disadvantage

any man who has not had
a not-much-talked about lunatic
among his ancestors
(preferably immediate)
is at a disadvantage
when it comes to understanding
the sudden, sourceless ferocities
of a lover's rage

Pity

I'm always saying, 'where's the time gone?'
Why can't a watch have pity
on a man?

Never

She watched him give his heart first, then his mind.
'He'll never make a poet,' she said. 'Too kind.'

and Testament

He enveloped the review, stuck it in the post.
'Well, that's him nailed to the mast
at last.'
When does a poet become a ghost?
How is a life's work laid to rest?

All that's left

'He's riddled with it,' she said.
'So all that's left to me
is the bit of elbow-grease in bed'.

He is

His smallish forehead is a global sea.
His mouth is music and his laugh
a child getting a Christmas gift.
He is a heart and a half.

In a moment

The girl's body leaves all cold behind.
A man's head, emerging, shields his eyes
from brightness, brightness of brightness.
In a moment, earth is paradise.

He taps his belly and

though beauty shines
      to stress the rot
he smells the air
      where she is not.

One day

The old killer does as he pleases.
He kneels to receive the blessings of roses.
One day he'll make a sacrifice of praise.

Mindbite

She looked to him like something to eat.
He changed his mind after one bite.

Another question

He'd read it hundreds of times before,
times he was weak, times he was strong.
He'd lost it every time, found it now
in one luminous moment. For how long?

Never knew why

As he was being mugged he thought
(never knew why he thought)
of Saint Michael letting the devil have it
in a lonely chapel among trees
where it seemed possible to believe
in Five Glorious Mysteries.

Bastard

Do people read poetry or does poetry
read people? Sally Jokeman-Whyte
says a poem is a bastard in a balaclava helmet
rapping your head in the middle of the night.
Next morning your ear is burned out.

Almost

The one-legged pigeon wins the crust.
I almost taste
love lost.

Unbungling

He unbungled his wife and hit the road
saluting as he went
several familiar
children of God.

True to birth

Stunted and wrinkled, he drags himself along.
Born a vagabond, still is, always will be,
world without end. His true friend
is any old train station. He's fifty, looks
eighty. He kisses total strangers
and never gives a reason.

A Radford slant on ageing

'Retrospection is an art, sharp and debonair.
I recognise the golden years
by the silver in my hair.'

Ever, never

The shyest man she ever met
became, pen in hand, the kind of snake
she'd never forget.
A shy snake's poison, like great art,
goes straight to the heart.

One bite

The shy snake is too polite
ever to give more than one bite.

It must, however, be conceded
one bite is all that's needed.

Birth

The moment he glimpsed the cat under the tree
waiting patiently, most patiently,
he knew it was himself he was looking at
because that was the birth of his lifestrong desire
to sink his teeth deep
into a neighbouring smartalec rat.

I remember, I remember

When the shy snake hisses
I remember certain kisses.

On the way

A gentle voice is music on the phone:
'I'm coming along the quays in the rain.'

Leafy fall

The stranger stays inside, hates to go out
in the leafy fall of the year.
People don't invite him either.
His brother is his enemy,
his enemy his brother.

Above the house

You call it yellow, I call it gold.
The angel's eyes will never grow old
and high above the house where the tipsy girl sings
the prisoner's dreams touch the angel's wings.

Epic

She told him the plot of the novel then
and gave sound reasons why it would sell,
the chief one being that the story resembled
epic masturbation in a prison cell.

The subject

She has noticed that when the subject comes up
                    it's always the killjoy
who spends the most money.
She smiles when the investment banker
                    knocks on her door.
For once, he's the customer.

Climber

A man entering politics is a man
climbing
                    into a garbage can.

Post-Futurism

Hamlet enters, stands alone.
'Fuck that mobile phone!'

Meeting-point

When poet and philosopher meet to speak
of poetry and revolution
a young man tells other young men
how to make a fortune.

Heart and feathers

'That fella is enjoying himself,' she said
of the lark in the fairly clear air
singing his heart and feathers out
like a wrenboy without a care.

Inexplicable

To look suddenly at eyes
renowned for sourness
and glimpse inexplicable tenderness
is a gift like morning itself
after a sleepless night
in a merciless bed
listening to sounds and voices
shafting havoc through my head.

So old

Ice remembers what men forget.
God is so old
He's not born yet.

A picture

Calmly, she looks over her shoulder again
at a picture to put
the joy of heaven and the fear of God
in the hearts of men.
Then, looking straight ahead, she walks on
towards the bombed-out town.

Sigh

Memory is the mind's belly.
After the old poet's words eased out
his mind heaved a sigh.

An old novelist's change of style

Forgive me, darling. Yes, I am guilty
(as you say) of revelling in shit.
I promise never again to make love
in a flea-pit.

Full of it

Sex by remote control she'll never forget.
'I know what you mean but the grass is wet.
I love you for it
and you're full of it.'

Tramplers

Why do they trample
the innocent bicycle
chained peacefully
near the door of the Irish
Cancer Society?

The worst sin

He sings as he has always sung,
laughs as he has always laughed.
The worst sin I can commit, he says,
is not to follow my gift.
Small though it be
it's the one for me.

In darkness I see them

Strange how I am haunted by some
I haven't seen for fifty years
and will not see again:

in darkness I see them
laughing, crying, playing, reaching out their hands,
knowing I cannot touch them even as I
dreamdelight in old, lost friends,
shadows on an evening wall
sunlight dancing at my beck and call
although there's nobody at all.

Family matter

'That Christmas Day, he wanted to kill his father.
It was over a will and a patch of land.
Lucky for both, he left the house before dinner
and confessed everything to the first whore he could find.'

Greetings

A solitary condom, sad and crinkled
in the cobbles of Front Square
greets the bells greeting
Sunday morning air.

Most of all

'Did you enjoy the weekend, darling?:'
'I liked the drunkards in the dark, the light.
I loved the love that kept on threatening
but most of all I loved the fight.'

Present

His smile stresses his broken jaw,
a Christmas present
from the law.

Help

A creak in the floor where nobody walks,
cry in the night, boy singing in Grafton Street,
sound of the wind, changing faces in flames
help Martha Wain in her lonely fight.

At the gate

Words spat from the traveller's mouth
are mad leaves
clattering the wild October night.
He's an East wind chilling the island.

Waking up

It is the strangest way to wake up:
reach out your hand, nobody there, outside noise
being born, a word in the air like breath:
superfluous.

Out there

They're out there, the right ones,
graceful, precise ones, who will bring them home?
Sit and wait, open and ready, it may happen
or I may be dumb.

Flick

She's another goner.
His tongue flicks the air
like the shy snake's
after dinner.

Lines

As the Atlantic withdraws
the lines on the beach are fresh and ancient
as the lines on Maggie Daly's face.

130

Rebirth

In her condition she was used to fainting
but was reborn in anger
when superior George compared her

        to an unfinished painting.

Tommy Edwards

reads Erotic Writings By Women
scratches his balls and his head
writes to Pattie Grey tellling her
he may come near to loving her
when she's dead

Corner of Talkers

At the Corner of Talkers he says to the publican,
'We are born in others' pain and perish in our own.'

'And where did you get that from, you sonofagun?'
'I knew a woman stole it from a decent Englishman'.

Perspective

She photographed the Library from Rotten Row
one sweaty June afternoon.
'Perspective is all, darling,' she smiled
'like an unravelling honeymoon.'

Homo ludens

When arse-licking assassins play
the victim rôle
sympathy and admiration flow
from pole to pole.

Dancing still

Hamnet Sadler looked at the will, the bed.
'This could flare into war,' he said.

Robert Whattcoat considered the silver bowl.
'Judith loves it, she of the golden soul.'

All former wills were then revoked by Will.
The moon dancing that evening is dancing still.

One and only

Someone stole a darling snake
from our one and only Zoo.

Although we're never shy to speculate
we don't know who.

Obedience

The sun and moon obey his words,
Kings and Queens his silences.

Melting

Is it a lie? He'll never know.
She melts in his blood like Easter snow,
no melting into yes, yes into no.

Principles

He's giving a lecture on principles.
Kitty Flood in the third row begins to look sick.
She leans to her left, whispers in Moll Cully's ear,
'All his principles are in his prick.'

Therefore I am not

At thirty-five, he gave up trying to think
and became Head of a Global Control Bank.

Scarcity

To be a poet and strike it rich,
To be a lover and bed every bitch;
Twin fulfilments we'd all love dearly
Could we but learn to write more clearly.

Corner

at the corner of her mouth
two sharp little wrinkles
almost imperceptible
guarantee
mischief and beauty

Some

She's determined to explore
the bowels of the earth because, she says,
deep in these bowels she can forget
some of the shit on the surface.

Practice

Amid laughter and tears, under the tick-tock
gravity of the grandfather clock, she chirps
'Look! I'm practisin' my gears!'

The search

The story never gives up its search
for the storyteller, beginning
'The bride stepped naked out of the the church.'

Of useless men

'Men are useless!' she said, 'simply useless!
They can't! They simply can't!
I need a panther to lick my cunt!'

Bad rain

That was bad rain bad rain endless bad rain.
At the end of the second day she thought
'I believed I was necessary. I'm not.'

No doubt

In the knowing village of Castlerainbow
nobody doubts the whiteness of snow
or the dark magic of Monica Crowe.

New

Fear no more the noise of the boom
as you sit in your calm room.
The new Irish Whiskey is Eden Bliss.
Tigerpiss.

Merger

Two things, merging, seem
        a quiet road towards light:
                madness when you dream,
                        reason when you write.

Perfection

The genomic specialist lies still and warm
dreaming of the perfect worm.

Vision

The first time she saw him, he was a nail,
the second, a kitchen knife,
the third, a sledgehammer.
Now, she's having the time of her life.
He's a comforting murmur.

All her summers

That evening was all her summers.
She threw her husband out with the dishwater
and let her freedom sleep in the arms of banter.

Beyond his reach

He looked at his children, all nine.
Someone said they were his greatest works.
He thought of words and signs beyond his reach
and loved his children like he loved question-marks.

Certain days

He sips his whiskey, this late summer evening,
talking of good and evil, shadows flitting:
'There's no crime, however vile, that on certain days
I am not capable of committing.'

Always

He always had to have the last word.
As he lay dying, he farted.

October dark

'Bless my head.'
In October dark he did, God knows he did.
It was like breaking bread.
Dark is the light's pulsing blood.

Gambler

She's gambling with the darkness now
as she has always done.
When she shakes her hair like feisty rain
she'll win.

Opening

He opened the book, a letter fell out,
dated two and fifty years ago.
It began, 'My love, why do you hate me so?'

Black purse

She shuts the black purse, tucks it away.
God knows what may come from under her dress
some later day.

Exile

The Dalai Lama, exiled, fondles the beards
of the Papist and the Prod.
There's a smile on every face
and on the face of God.

Because of

I said good-bye to the stranger one morning
        when the air was blue
but then because of my empty mind I
        invited him back.
Back he came, talking his head off as usual,
this time about the way the sea gets picassoed
by a scarcely imaginable shipwreck.
He fell silent then, imitating a rock.

For what?

For what did the unknowns toil and bleed?
Speed. Greed. Speedgreed.

History

'Very few want to read history,' the teacher said.
'Greed is always staring straight ahead.'

Choice

'Milk or cream in your coffee, lad?'
'Whatever stops it tastin' bad.'

I stand

When love succumbs to light
    and locks the darkness out
I stand with gathered strangers
    at the christening of doubt.

Explorer

The magpie explores the cowdung
with the vigour of a lad firstnighting it
in the land of forever young.

The test

Slow waltzing will put Beethoven
to the test. She mesmerises all in the hall
as only a waltzing virgin can.

A wounded place

This is a wounded place.
As blood flows
from city town village field mountain glen,
nobody knows.
Wounds deepen as speedgreed grows.

Inflation

The unknowns enrich the grass,
inflate the bellies of the famous.

Facing the storm

the church made in the shape of a boat
faces the storm from all quarters,
finds it hard to stay afloat

The place

'I know the place well,' she said,
'badgers, rats, ferrets, bees
and a parish priest
adored by fleas.'

The beggar curses his mocker

May your arse fester
mortify and blister
shut up
and never again open.

Menu

The defendant eats a sardine.
His lawyer sniffs a salmon.
The judge orders more.
Prisons are for the poor.

Sprinklers

The young Moor sipping his Paddy
says of Nellie Kitt:
'I sprinkled her with rose water,
she sprinkled me with shit.'

Realisation

'The morning after he murdered my dream
I realised
shit never turns to cream.'

Hole

She knows she loves him day and night,
night and day, always, more and more.
            She'll give it to him
even through a hole in the door.

Spoilt

'Spoilt? Bet your life she's spoilt!
I sent her out to buy grapes.
She came back six months pregnant.'

Mitching

The leaf scuttles across the schoolyard
like a mitching lad with the helpless air
of one who can't avoid becoming
a dot com millionaire.

Investment

When the old gombeen buys a young wife
young men of the village rejoice.
They sniff his investment, like dogs their lice.

Garden

Afer the wedding she glimpsed herself
stretched in a garden in Sligo Grange.
She didn't like the way
her bones were arranged.

Stolen money

Stolen money softpedals the darkness
where a slim beauty dreams of being slimmer
and a slim man facing the door of hell
beats with a golden hammer.

Cartel

Crime in the street
cannot compete
with crime in the suite.
'We love competitors. Customers we hate.'

I asked

What turns Parnassus into a mountain of hate?
I asked Percy, William, Emily, John.
Open minds know when to keep their mouths shut.

Of non-existence

'He doesn't exist in law,' the judge said.
'A shadowless man is William Magee.
Therefore, he cannot be charged.
Let the shadowless man go free.'

Company

'I love the company of prophets,' she said,
        'they put scribblers to shame.
I will be read,' she said,
        'in a hundred years time.
Then why has daddy
        forgotten my name?'

Poor man wondering

She was so pharmaceutically demure
as she handed the bottle to the poor man
he wondered, 'Is this a cure
or a poison?'

To a young writer

Cry, if you will. I'd say, though, rather than
tears, shed a few smiles around the town.
You must be talented, young man.
The knifey bunch are out to cut you down.

To an old writer

What is it you saw inside
when the holy door
opened wide?

Slipping on his coat, he said

'When I was a slave, I made money.
Now that I'm free, I enjoy
the company of slaves.'

True and false

After decades in the whirling thick
of the moneyjungle, he loves, most of all,
his silver toothpick

though his teeth are false.

Right

'The time is right,' she said. 'Come on, come on,
        be crushingly beautiful.
                I carried a calf.
                        I can bear the bull.'

Itch

Although the sun is the cloak of the poor
this porcupine castrator
itches all over.

End of the lane

The old century lay down in the shed
at the end of the lane:
'Here's to a long rest, God bless the dead,
I'll not trouble you again.'

Time no time

When the sun sinks the moon grins.
Hope is sleeping in litter-bins.

Tricks

Whiskey plays tricks on its lovers.
How many lizards
wriggle out through his fingers?

Whistler

She had no reputation for lust.
Nobody ever called her a whore
but she'd laugh at any man's best
and whistle for more.

No return

When the curse goes out, the curse stays out.
Spit never returns to the mouth.
If another spit is needed the mouth provides it.

A mad attack

Bless them that curse you, he said.
Curses spat on her head like a mad attack
of rain. She dodged and danced and walked away
with her good name.

If I must

If I must choose, then let it be
the blown, magnanimous cherrytree,
cherrysnow on open ground,
a scientist pondering, head down.

Order of merit

He celebrates the widow's dips and curves.
Every village has the Shakespeare it deserves.

So many things

Skeletons suss clever flesh,
heaven educates, learns from hell;
so many things tight-lipped
poems won't tell.

Odyssey

She trudged a long way through mucky fields to feed birds.
She heard them singing afterwards.

Shock Sexchange

On opening night she kneels to pray
for bullish results on closing day.

His own songs

A man who knows the streets and speaks to angels
says this education is a sin
mis-shaping many a girl and boy.
He'll die singing his own songs
of praise and joy.

From a Galway woman

Sing it clearly as you can
and if you reach the heights
share the mountain
with your neighbours.

Muddy water

Leave the muddy water alone, she said.
Don't go too near, don't meddle,
it'll make itself clear.

Clockwise

Turn me on, dear, turn me on.
I'll be ticking gladly
when you're gone.

Wanting

When the sickness struck, the words died.
The stranger slumped in a heap in the yard.
I was mud again, heavy blue mud.
But I licked it, I licked the mud
and came back, weaker, wanting to work hard
or fling it all to the mad, vicious winds of God.

Cover

When money strays he brings it home
and buys what it takes to cover his shame.
One may sell a soul to buy a name.

Challenges

More challenging than an empty page
is a woman's body full of rage.

The joy

She looks, sees a face that loves being adored.
She walks down Flame Street, crosses a bridge,
savours the joy of being ignored.

Conversation

Half-way through the conversation he glimpsed
his life's greatest mistake.
For a cutting moment he was wideawake.
How long did the moment last? Enough to make
a spirit shake.

Red candle

Where the red candle burns, pigeons alight on bread,
a Jew and an Arab strip for bed,
a tomtit chirps a frosty accolade.

Planets

Together in bed, they're planets apart.
She's in the arms of Jupiter.
He's chatting with Mars.

Consciousness

Back from Africa, she says she's conscious of the fact
she'll be reviled
for saying she'd burn every poem ever written
if it meant she could feed a starving child.

Traffic lights

He reached out, grabbed the child at the traffic-lights.
Twenty years later, a woman thanked him
in a wintry street.

Cold

The boy's hands are blue with cold.
Ice grips young blood.
The forecast is not good.

On the road

'The fascination of flesh,' the stranger said, 'lies in the fact
that it's potentially rotten.
Beauty is a glimpse on the road to putrefaction.'

Funny

Corruption rhymes with Dublin
in a funny sort of way.
Listen to what blood factors say.
Relax. Enjoy the funny, stinking play.

On trial

We hold our breath, the island is on trial.
From Ballybeg to Clonakilty
of the noble black pudding
the flesh becomes word: guilty.

Reminder

Colours switching on the pigeon's neck
remind me of your winning trick.

Nightflowers

'I know you'll laugh at this, me love,' she said,
'but last night, while our wild music lasted
and our hearts banished all the usual fears
I could feel flowers growin' outa me ears.'

The Muse

He takes Shelley from the shelf,
lets the West Wind rip his head.
He gets horny over poems
while the wife snores in bed.

Bad

She looked at the scuttery shit in the bed.
'Didn't I tell you I was a bad Catholic?' he said.

What it takes

Take a deep breath before you drop the bomb.
That's what it takes to rubbish the claim,
I am.

Two

Two possible definitions of hell:
one, the stories nobody will tell;
two, maybe it's just as well.

Every step

Cold, at the edges of the flesh, the stranger
heads for home, wherever that is.
I think it haunts every step he takes
and with every step he takes, home changes.

Fool

The day I knew my world is one of glimpses
I felt something of a fool.
Then I asked myself if anyone has ever
seen anybody whole.

The hunt

A poem is a greyhound chasing a hare
that may not be there
at all. According to greyhound lovers
it's the hunt that matters.

Together

Bring a fool and a hunt together
you'll have anything
from fun to murder.

Knowing not knowing

'If you know you don't know,' she said,
'you tend to have laughing eyes.
Give the past a chance,' she said,
'give the present a helping hand,
give the future a surprise.'

Playtime

'You're my hypnotic, indecisive one.'

'And you're my perfumed, fleshed out skeleton.'

Street-talkers

'They're pourin' plaudits on his head.'

'Jaysus, he must be dead!'

At moments

In early spring, she writes to her lover
on the backs of leaves
as Maoris did at moments of danger.

Deep night

In the deep night of epiphany
can it be that the demon yearns
for peace or the reward of loneliness
when the red candle burns?

That happy moment

In that happy moment when loving bodies tire
the demon cut my throat
with a knife of fire.

In the nearby lake of blazing water
loving bodies
scavenged and ate each other.

According to plan

He said he'd hang himself. He did.
A frosty morning. He was one wild man.
Everything went according to plan.

You could tell

She looked at the corpse laid out in the bed.
'God bless him, he's lookin' so well
you could tell
he's just back from his holiday,' she said.

Scuttlers

She thinks of Simon's flattering croon
when she sees clouds
pay scuttling homage to the moon.

Breaking the wall

Shifting always, tide of truth and lies,
battering ram that breaks the wall
blocking my eyes.

Fallout

If I shake myself
like an old overcoat

who knows what'll fall out?

Still to be done

Tiredness hits him, failure snuggles in close,
years of work stalk him, bleating
and slipping. One thing he knows, one thing.
Everything is still to be done. Everything.

Brendan Kennelly was born in 1936 in Ballylongford, Co. Kerry; and was educated at St Ita's College, Tarbert, Co. Kerry, and at Trinity College, Dublin, where he has been Professor of Modern Literature since 1973. He has published more than twenty books of poems, including six volumes of selected poems, most recently *A Time for Voices: Selected Poems 1960-1990* (Bloodaxe, 1990) and *Breathing Spaces: Early Poems* (Bloodaxe, 1992). His latest books are *The Man Made of Rain* (Bloodaxe, 1998), written after he survived major heart surgery (available in hardback and paperback editions as well as on a double-cassette tape), and two new collections, *Begin* (Bloodaxe, 1999) and *Glimpses* (Bloodaxe, 2001).

He is best-known for two controversial poetry books, *Cromwell*, published in Ireland in 1983 and in Britain by Bloodaxe in 1987, and his epic poem *The Book of Judas*, (Bloodaxe, 1991), which topped the Irish bestsellers list: a shorter version will appear from Bloodaxe in 2002 as *The Little Book of Judas*. His third epic, *Poetry My Arse* (Bloodaxe, 1995), did much to outdo these in notoriety.

His translations of Irish poetry are available in *Love of Ireland: Poems from the Irish* (Mercier Press, 1989). He has edited several anthologies, including *The Penguin Book of Irish Verse* (1970; 2nd edition 1981), *Between Innocence and Peace: Favourite Poems of Ireland* (Mercier Press, 1993), *Ireland's Women: Writings Past and Present*, with Katie Donovan and A. Norman Jeffares (Gill & Macmillan, 1994), and *Dublines*, with Katie Donovan (Bloodaxe Books, 1995). He has published two novels, *The Crooked Cross* (1963) and *The Florentines* (1967).

He is also a celebrated dramatist whose plays include versions of *Antigone* (Peacock Theatre, Dublin, 1986; Bloodaxe, 1996); *Medea*, premièred in the Dublin Theatre Festival in 1988, toured in England in 1989 by the Medea Theatre Company, and broadcast by BBC Radio 3 and published by Bloodaxe in 1991; *The Trojan Women* (Peacock Theatre & Bloodaxe, 1993); and Lorca's *Blood Wedding* (Northern Stage, Newcastle & Bloodaxe, 1996).

His *Journey into Joy: Selected Prose*, edited by Åke Persson, was published by Bloodaxe in 1994, along with *Dark Fathers into Light*, a critical anthology on his work edited by Richard Pine. Åke Persson has also published *That Fellow with the Fabulous Smile: A Tribute to Brendan Kennelly* (Bloodaxe, 1996).

His cassette recordings include *The Man Made of Rain* (Bloodaxe, 1998) and *The Poetry Quartets: 4*, shared with Paul Durcan, Michael Longley and Medbh McGuckian (The British Council / Bloodaxe Books, 1999).